ANIMALS THAT LIVE ON THE FARM
ANIMALES QUE VIVEN EN LA GRANJA

Cows/ Las vacas

JoAnn Early Macken

Reading consultant/Consultora de lectura:
Susan Nations, M.Ed.,
author/literacy coach/consultant

WEEKLY WR READER®
EARLY LEARNING LIBRARY

Please visit our web site at: www.earlyliteracy.cc
For a free color catalog describing Weekly Reader® Early Learning Library's list
of high-quality books, call 1-877-445-5824 (USA) or 1-800-387-3178 (Canada).
Weekly Reader® Early Learning Library's fax: (414) 336-0164.

Library of Congress Cataloging-in-Publication Data

Macken, JoAnn Early, 1953-
    (Cows. Spanish & English)
    Cows = Las vacas / JoAnn Early Macken.
      p. cm. — (Animals that live on the farm = Animales que viven en la granja)
    Includes bibliographical references and index.
    ISBN 0-8368-4286-3 (lib. bdg.)
    ISBN 0-8368-4293-6 (softcover)
    1. Dairy cattle—Juvenile literature. 2. Cows—Juvenile literature.
    I. Title: Vacas. II. Title.
SF208.M2418 2004
636.2—dc22
                                        2004054961

This edition first published in 2005 by
Weekly Reader® Early Learning Library
330 West Olive Street, Suite 100
Milwaukee, WI 53212 USA

Picture research: Diane Laska-Swanke
Art direction: Tammy West
Cover design and page layout: Kami Strunsee
Translators: Colleen Coffey and Consuelo Carrillo

Photo credits: Cover, pp. 7, 11, 13, 15, 17, 19 Gregg Andersen;
pp. 5, 9 © Alan & Sandy Carey; p. 21 © James P. Rowan

Printed in the United States of America

2 3 4 5 6 7 8 9 10 09 08 07 06

Note to Educators and Parents

Reading is such an exciting adventure for young children! They are beginning to integrate their oral language skills with written language. To encourage children along the path to early literacy, books must be colorful, engaging, and interesting; they should invite the young reader to explore both the print and the pictures.

Animals That Live on the Farm is a new series designed to help children read about the behavior and life cycles of farm animals. Each book describes a different type of animal and explains why and how it is raised.

Each book is specially designed to support the young reader in the reading process. The familiar topics are appealing to young children and invite them to read — and re-read — again and again. The full-color photographs and enhanced text further support the student during the reading process.

In addition to serving as wonderful picture books in schools, libraries, homes, and other places where children learn to love reading, these books are specifically intended to be read within an instructional guided reading group. This small group setting allows beginning readers to work with a fluent adult model as they make meaning from the text. After children develop fluency with the text and content, the book can be read independently. Children and adults alike will find these books supportive, engaging, and fun!

Una nota a los educadores y a los padres

¡La lectura es una emocionante aventura para los niños! En esta etapa están comenzando a integrar su manejo del lenguaje oral con el lenguaje escrito. Para fomentar la lectura desde una temprana edad, los libros deben ser vistosos, atractivos e interesantes; deben invitar al joven lector a explorar tanto el texto como las ilustraciones.

Animales que viven en la granja es una nueva serie pensada para ayudar a los niños a conocer la conducta y los ciclos de vida de los animales de la granja. Cada libro describe un tipo diferente de animal y explica por qué y cómo se cria.

Cada libro ha sido especialmente diseñado para facilitar el proceso de lectura. La familiaridad con los temas tratados atrae la atención de los niños y los invita a leer — y releer — una y otra vez. Las fotografías a todo color y el tipo de letra facilitan aún más al estudiante el proceso de lectura.

Además de servir como fantásticos libros ilustrados en la escuela, la biblioteca, el hogar y otros lugares donde los niños aprenden a amar la lectura, estos libros han sido concebidos específicamente para ser leídos en grupos de instrucción guiada. Este contexto de grupos pequeños permite que los niños que se inician en la lectura trabajen con un adulto cuya fluidez les sirve de modelo para comprender el texto. Una vez que se han familiarizado con el texto y el contenido, los niños pueden leer los libros por su cuenta. ¡Tanto niños como adultos encontrarán que estos libros son útiles, entretenidos y divertidos!

— Susan Nations, M.Ed., author, literacy coach,
and consultant in literacy development

Cows are female cattle.
Bulls are male cattle. A
baby cow is called a **calf**.

— — — — — — — —

Las vacas son las hembras
del ganado. Los toros son
los machos del ganado.
La vaca joven se llama
ternera.

A calf can stand soon after it is born. It drinks milk from its mother.

- - - - - - - -

Al poco tiempo de nacer, el ternero se puede sostener en pie. Se alimenta con la leche de la madre.

In warm weather, cows stay outside. They graze on grass. They swish their tails to flick away flies.

- - - - - - - -

Cuando hace calor, las vacas se quedan fuera del establo. Pastan la hierba. Dan latigazos con la cola para espantar las moscas.

Cows lie down to rest. They face away from the wind.

Las vacas se echan para descansar. Le dan la espalda al viento.

In cold weather, cows stay in a barn. Most farmers feed cows hay, corn, and oats.

— — — — — — —

Cuando hace frío las vacas se quedan en el establo. La mayoría de los granjeros alimentan las vacas con heno, maíz y avena.

After a cow eats, it burps up its food. Then it chews the food again. The food it chews is called its **cud**.

\- \- \- \- \- \- \- \-

Después de que la vaca come, vuelve a la boca el alimento. Luego rumia la comida otra vez. La comida que mastica se llama **bolo alimenticio**.

Cows spend most of the day eating or chewing. They drink lots of water every day.

- - - - - - - -

Las vacas pasan la mayoría del día comiendo o rumiando. Beben mucha agua todos los días.

Farmers keep cows for meat and milk. Farmers milk the cows twice a day.

— — — — — — — —

Los granjeros crían las vacas para carne y leche. Ordeñan la leche de las vacas dos veces al día.

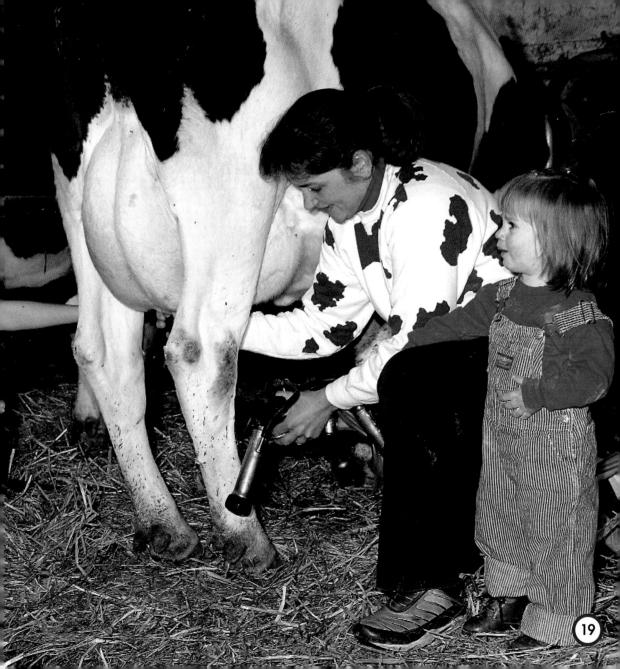

Some people use cattle to pull heavy loads. Have you ever seen cows on a farm?

– – – – – – – –

Hay gente que usa el ganado para halar carga pesada. ¿Alguna vez has visto vacas en una granja?

Glossary/Glosario

cattle — animals such as oxen or cows that chew their cud and are kept on a farm or a ranch
ganado — animales como bueyes o vacas que rumian el bolo alimenticio y que se mantienen en una granja o una hacienda

graze — to eat grass
pastar — comer hierba

hay — grass that is cut and dried for food
heno — hierba que se corta y se seca para comida

For More Information/Más información

Books/Libros

Cow. Malachy Doyle (Margaret K. McElderry)

Cow. Jules Older (Charlesbridge)

Kiss the Cow. Phyllis Root (Candlewick)

Milk. Where Does Our Food Come From?
(series). Gretchen Will Mayo (Weekly Reader
Early Learning Library)

Web Sites/Páginas Web

Got Milk?
www.got-milk.com/
Cow and milk facts, games, and recipes

Index/Índice

About the Author/Información sobre la autora

JoAnn Early Macken is the author of two rhyming picture books, *Sing-Along Song* and *Cats on Judy*, and four other series of nonfiction books for beginning readers. Her poems have appeared in several children's magazines. A graduate of the M.F.A. in Writing for Children and Young Adults program at Vermont College, she lives in Wisconsin with her husband and their two sons. Visit her Web site at www.joannmacken.com.

JoAnn Early Macken es autora de dos libros infantiles ilustrados en verso, *Sing-Along Song* y *Cats on Judy*, y también de cuatro series de libros de corte realista dirigidos a los lectores principiantes. Sus poemas han sido publicados en varias revistas para niños. Graduada del M.F.A. en Redacción para niños y adultos jóvenes del Vermont College, vive en Wisconsin con su esposo y sus dos hijos. Visita su página Web. www.joannmacken.com.